CW00404538

Don't miss...

Where do you want to go?

You choose...

Nature's Cathedral 2

BLUE ZONE
Dinosaurs 6
Human Biology 10
Mammals 12
Fishes, Amphibians and Reptiles 16
Marine Invertebrates 18

GREEN ZONE
Minerals and The Vault 20
Creepy Crawlies 22
Fossil Marine Reptiles 24
Birds 26

RED ZONE
Primates 28
Earth Hall 30
Volcanoes and Earthquakes 32
Restless Surface 34
Earth's Treasury 36
From the Beginning 38

ORANGE ZONE
Incredible Collections 40
Super Science 42

More about the Museum 44
Answers 46

Nature's Cathedral

Step inside one of London's most amazing buildings.

What makes the Museum look like a cathedral?

The Natural History Museum was built in the 1870s. The building is decorated with tiles and features made of baked clay, called terracotta. What other features make it look like a cathedral?

Imilac

This gem-filled meteorite is more than 4.5 billion years old, and dates from the very dawn of our solar system. Scientists think that the Imilac meteorite is part of a much larger meteor that exploded over the Atacama Desert in northern Chile. It is the oldest item on display in Hintze Hall.

Blue marlin

The blue marlin is one of the largest and fastest fish in the ocean. It spends most of its life far out at sea but, although the ocean is deep, it prefers the warm water near the surface. This incredible solitary predator feeds on mackerel and tuna, but also dives deep to eat squid. It uses its long, spear-shaped rostrum, studded with thousands of conical teeth, to slash through schools of fish. This 4 metre long blue marlin, which is on display in Hintze Hall, was found washed up on a South Wales beach in September 2016.

Mastodon

The Museum bought this American mastodon in 1844. These ancient relatives of the elephant roamed North America until approximately 13,000 years ago. This magnificent vegetarian probably ate a mixture of bark, leaves and grass. Scientists think that it went extinct because of climate change, habitat loss and hunting by humans.

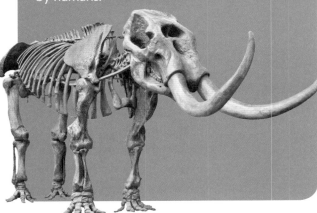

Seaweed

There are three different kinds of seaweed: brown, red and green. They are often found washed up on beaches. Seaweed is vital for marine life. Like plants on land they photosynthesize converting carbon dioxide to oxygen. Marine animals depend on seaweed for this oxygen, as well as for food and a place to live.

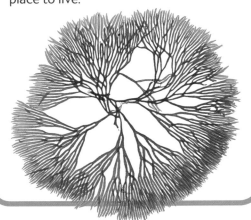

Blue whale skeleton

Look up at the skeleton of Hope, a huge female blue whale diving above you. The whale was stranded in Ireland in 1891, ten years after the Museum opened. Its skeleton was bought by the Museum and first went on display in the Mammal Hall in 1938. While staff were moving the whale to Hintze Hall they discovered some copies of a newspaper called the *Kent Messenger*. The newspaper was used to hold some of the 220 bones together.

Explore the displays around Hintze Hall and see some of the Museum's special specimens.

Nature's Cathedral

Home to more than 80 million objects.

Find the display of specimen collectors and explorers on the balconies.

Birds

You can see that the male common pheasant is more colourful and larger than the female. This difference is common in birds between males and females of the same species. Spot more male and female birds like this in the Bird Balcony display.

Painted plants

Look up at the ceiling in Hintze Hall. Can you see the panels showing different kinds of plants? This one shows the seed pods of the cacao plant from which chocolate is made.

Alfred Waterhouse

The Museum was designed by a young architect from Liverpool called Alfred Waterhouse. He sketched every one of the animal and plant sculptures and carvings – a mixture of extinct and living species – that you can see throughout the building.

Giraffe

The giraffe's neck makes it the tallest living animal, and has the same number of bones as a human's neck – seven. But the giraffe's neck bones are much longer. Their long necks mean they can reach and feed on tall bushes and shrubs beyond the reach of other animals.

A **giraffe's tongue** can grow to a whopping 53 cm!

I spy terracotta

How many of these clay creatures can you spot on the walls inside and outside the Museum building?

bat kangaroo
lion monkey octopus
owl pterosaur

The biggest living thing

The Museum looks after a slice of a giant sequoia trunk. The giant sequoia from California, USA is the world's largest living thing because of its bulk. One of its relatives, the coast redwood, is the tallest tree.

How old?
The tree was a seedling in the year 557. How old was the tree when it was cut down in 1892?

Dinosaurs

Come face to face with some of the scariest animals that ever lived on land.

Did you know, the word dinosaur means 'terrible reptile'.

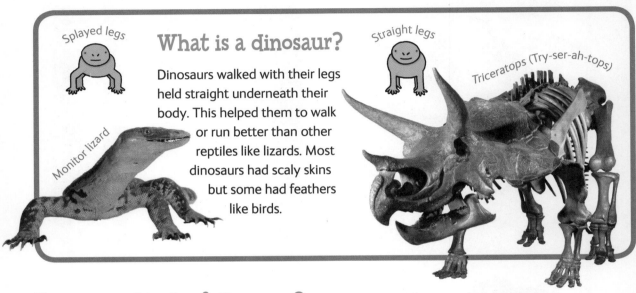

Splayed legs

What is a dinosaur?

Straight legs

Triceratops (Try-ser-ah-tops)

Dinosaurs walked with their legs held straight underneath their body. This helped them to walk or run better than other reptiles like lizards. Most dinosaurs had scaly skins but some had feathers like birds.

Monitor lizard

How many kinds of dinosaur?

Scientists have discovered about 1,000 different kinds of dinosaur. Over half of these are known only from a few of their fossil bones. But the Museum's *Stegosaurus* is made up of over 90 per cent original fossil pieces, making it a very rare specimen. Scientists still discover new kinds of dinosaur today by digging up new fossils and by studying fossil specimens in museum collections.

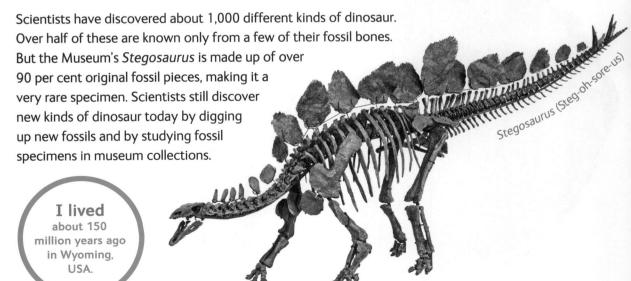

Stegosaurus (Steg-oh-sore-us)

I lived about 150 million years ago in Wyoming, USA.

Small ones

Velociraptor (Vel-oh-see-rap-tuh) was about the height of a large dog. They hunted in packs to bring down prey larger than themselves. The smallest dinosaurs were about the size of a chicken and ate small prey, such as insects.

Two feet or four feet

The biggest dinosaurs plodded along on four feet. They had pillar-like legs to support their bulky bodies. The fastest dinosaurs ran along on two legs. *Gallimimus* (Gal-lee-meem-us) was a fast runner that used speed to escape danger. *Iguanodon* (Ig-wha-noh-don) could walk on four feet and may have also stood up on its back legs like a bear.

Can you find me in the Dinosaur gallery?

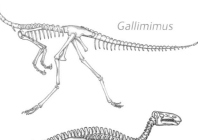

Gallimimus

Iguanodon

Diplodocus

Dinosaur alphabet

There is a dinosaur name for every letter of the alphabet. Fill them in – for help visit our Dino Directory at www.nhm.ac.uk/dino-directory.

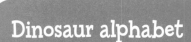

A _ l _ a _ _ s
B _ r _ o _ x
C _ _ l _ p _ _ s _ s
D _ i _ c _ _ _ r _ s
E _ _ o _ o _ _ _ us
F _ _ _ _ r _ p _ or
G _ l _ _ _ _ us
H y _ _ _ l _ _ _ d _ n
I _ _ _ n _ _ n

J _ n _ n _ c _ i _
K _ n t _ _ s _ _ r _ _
L a _ b _ osa _ _ _ s
M _ _ _ _ _ _ r _
N _ d _ era _ _ _ _
O _ _ r _ p _ _ r
P _ c _ y _ _ p _ _ _ o _ a _ r _ s
Q u _ _ _ t _ _ a r _ s
R _ g _ p _

S a _ t _ _ _ s
T _ _ _ n n _ s _ _ r _ s
U _ a _ r _ p _ or
V _ _ _ c _ r _ _ _ or
W i n _ _ _ ot _ t _ n
X _ a _ t _ n _ i _
Y _ n _ _ n _
Z a _ _ _ x _ s

Dinosaurs

Discover what scientists learn about the lives of dinosaurs by studying their fossils.

Veggies

Some dinosaurs, called herbivores, only ate plants. The large, long-necked dinosaurs had raking teeth to tear off leaves from the treetops. To grind the leaves up, they swallowed stones that churned around in their stomachs. Other plant-eating dinosaurs had multiple rows of grinding teeth.

Raking front teeth of *Diplodocus* (Dip-low-dock-us)

Grinding teeth of *Edmontosaurus* (Ed-mont-oh-sore-us)

Dinosaur stomach stones

Noisy neighbours

Parasaurolophus, (Par-ah-sore-ol-oh-fus) could warn others in its herd of danger by blowing air through the crest on its head. This made a low trumpeting sound.

Marvellous mums

All dinosaurs laid eggs like birds. Some baby dinosaurs were able to run about soon after hatching. Others, such as *Maiasaura* (My-ah-sore-ah), needed to be looked after for some time by their mothers.

Bony heads

Scientists think that male *Pachycephalosaurus* (Pack-ee-keff-ah-low-sore-us) head-butted each other in competition over females. Their thick bony skulls probably protected their rather small brains.

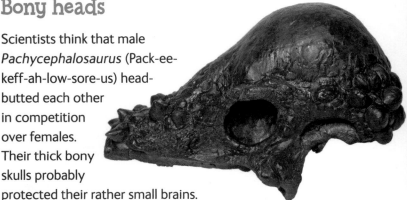

Meet me for lunch

Do you think *Tyrannosaurus* (Tie-ran-oh-sore-us) was a blood-thirsty hunter or do you think it scavenged from carcasses of dead animals? The chances are it may have done both. What we know for certain is that its jaws were strong and armed with sharp curved teeth that stopped victims from escaping. They could easily crunch through flesh and bones.

Thumb of *Iguanodon*

Heads or tails?

Plant-eating dinosaurs had to defend themselves from the fierce meat-eaters. *Triceratops* had a heavy, bony head-shield and impressive horns. *Euoplocephalus* swung the bony club at the end of its tail to knock out its enemies. *Iguanodon* may have hit out with its spiked thumb.

Tail of *Euoplocephalus*

Where did dinosaurs go?

Dinosaurs ruled the Earth for 150 million years. They all disappeared 66 million years ago. What do you think finished them off? It could have been gas and chemicals from volcanoes, or a gigantic asteroid hitting Earth from space.

Match the heads

Scientists rarely find the complete skeleton of a dinosaur in one place. Our dinosaur skeletons are missing their skulls. Draw a line between the correct skull and its body.

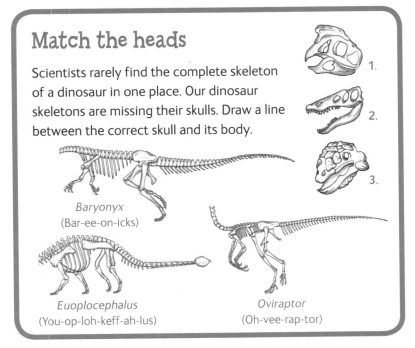

1.

2.

3.

Baryonyx
(Bar-ee-on-icks)

Euoplocephalus
(You-op-loh-keff-ah-lus)

Oviraptor
(Oh-vee-rap-tor)

Human Biology

Time to learn what makes you tick!

What kind of joint lets you bend at the knees?

What is the smallest part of you?

Like other living things, the smallest part of your body is a single cell. Your body has 50 million, million cells! There are many different cells, such as muscle and nerve cells. Most cells have a nucleus that holds strands of DNA containing sets of instructions, called genes. One set of genes is what makes your eyes brown or blue.

A long strand of DNA

Getting it together

Cells work together in groups, called tissues. Muscle is one kind of tissue. Each muscle cell is long and thin. Within the cell are minute strands that contract and relax. Many bundles of muscle cells make up each muscle.

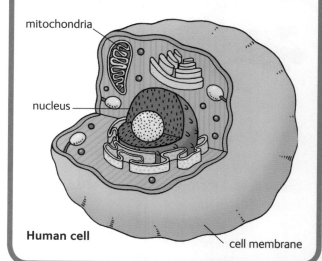

mitochondria

nucleus

Human cell

cell membrane

Making a baby

A new life begins when the dad's sperm meets the mum's egg inside her womb. The fertilized egg divides many times, making more and more cells. Gradually, the baby starts to grow. After seven months, the baby looks like this. It will be another two months before the baby is born.

Can you hear a baby's heartbeat when it is in its mother's womb?

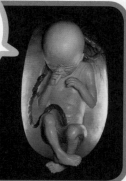

Brilliant brain

A human brain is amazing. While you read this, it is taking signals from your eyes and making sense of them. When you turn the page, the brain sends signals along the nerves to trigger the muscles in your hand.

A real human brain and spinal cord

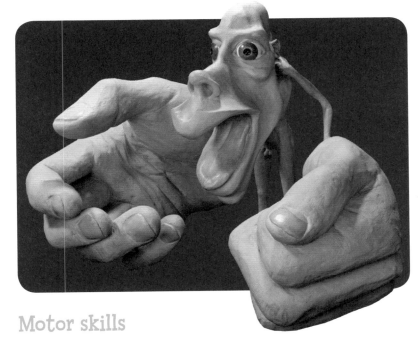

Motor skills

This strange model shows how much of the brain is used to control the movement of different parts of the body. The hands are huge because a large part of the brain is used to control their movement. This is one reason why you can hold a pencil and text on a mobile phone.

Pulling power

Your muscles can only pull on your bones, they cannot push them. Muscles like the biceps and triceps work in pairs. One muscle pulls, the other relaxes. When you bend your arm, the biceps muscle is pulling. To straighten your arm, the triceps muscle is pulling.

What do you see?

Your brain tries to make sense of the things you see, using memories of what you have seen before. Sometimes, it can get very confused!

 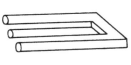 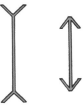

1. Is it a duck or a rabbit?

2. Is it a three-pronged object?

3. Which line is longest?

Mammals

See marvelous mammals from the present and the past.

Spot *Diprotodon* in the gallery – the largest marsupial that ever lived.

What is a mammal?

Mammal mothers suckle their young on milk. Mammals have a variety of lifestyles from high-flying bats to deep-diving whales. Most mammals have fur or hair. They usually sweat to keep themselves cool. You are a mammal.

Egg-layer

The platypus lays eggs instead of giving birth to live young. Platypus hunt for their food in the water where they live. They use their bill-like snout to detect electrical signals from worms, snails and other small prey. The male platypus is one of the few mammals that is venomous.

Bottoms up

The three-banded armadillo has body armour made of bony plates. When danger approaches, it rolls up into a ball. The fairy armadillo only has bony plates on its back. It escapes danger by burrowing but leaves its bottom sticking out, so the bony plates block the entrance to the burrow.

Three-banded armadillo

Sloth

African grassland

Jerboa

Himalayan mountains

South American swamp

Where do I live?

Match the mammal to where it lives.

Lion

Snow leopard

South American rainforest

Capybara

Sahara desert

What is the proper name for a mammal that has a pouch?

m _ _ _ u _ _ _ _

In the pouch

Kangaroos carry their young in a pouch. When it is born, the joey (the baby kangaroo) is the size of a jelly bean. The tiny baby crawls into the pouch where it suckles.

Are mammals dying out today?

Mammals are threatened by over-hunting and destruction of their homes in the wild. Another major threat is climate change. For example, rising temperatures mean Arctic sea ice is disappearing. Polar bears depend on the sea ice as a base to hunt seals from. Because there is less sea ice and it is melting earlier each year, the bears have less time to hunt.

Mammals

Meet the blue whale and other magnificent mammals.

How do large mammals support their weight?

Heavy land mammals, such as elephants and rhinoceroses, have pillar-like legs with big foot pads to support their weight. Whales can grow so large because the water supports their weight. They are crushed by their own weight if they come ashore.

Count my toes

Many plant-eating mammals have hooves instead of claws. Some of these mammals have two or four toes, which are even numbers. The camel above has two toes. Others, like zebra, have one toe, some have three, which are odd numbers.

Odds on

Fit the names of these odd-toed hoofed mammals into the puzzle:
donkey, horse, rhinoceros, tapir, zebra

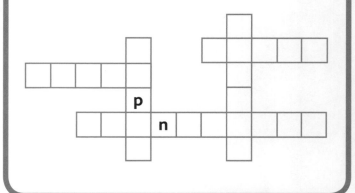

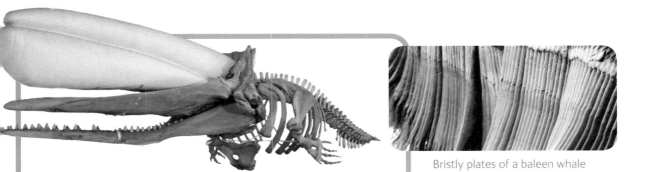

Bristly plates of a baleen whale

Skeleton of a toothed sperm whale

What is a whale?

Whales have flippers and a tail made up of two flukes that have no bones. Baleen whales have bristly plates in their mouths to catch food. Other whales, dolphins and porpoises have teeth instead, like the sperm whale skeleton above. The organs that are important in the production of sound have been added to this skeleton (white areas).

Blue giant

The blue whale is the largest animal that ever lived. It is bigger than the largest dinosaur. The blue whale can weigh up to 150 tonnes. Our famous blue whale was modelled on a beached whale so it is not as sleek as the living animal.

Climb the stairs to the balcony in Hintze Hall to get a fabulous view of Hope the blue whale.

Echoes

Toothed whales and dolphins can sense what is around them using sound. They send out high-pitched sounds, which bounce off things in front of them. The time it takes for the echoes to come back tells the whale or dolphin how far away something is.

Fishes, Amphibians and Reptiles

Can you spot the differences between a sea turtle and a land tortoise?

Get to know some weird and wonderful cold-blooded creatures.

What is a fish?

Fishes have fins, live in water and take in oxygen through their gills. Bony fishes usually have scales and their gills are covered by a flap. Sharks have gill slits and gristle-like cartilage instead of bone. There are more kinds of fishes than all the other animals with backbones put together.

What is an amphibian?

Frogs, salamanders and newts are among the different kinds of amphibians. The adults live on land but lay their eggs in water or damp places. Most adult amphibians have lungs but they all breathe through their skins.

Spot the difference

Can you spot the four differences between these two clown fish?

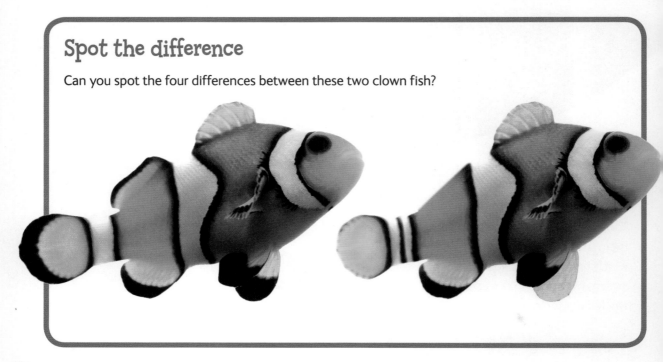

Tortoises have a bony shell covered in horny scales

What is a reptile?

Turtles, tortoises, snakes, lizards and crocodiles are all reptiles. They have dry scaly skins and usually lay eggs on land. Many kinds of reptiles bask in the Sun to warm up. Snakes are legless reptiles that have a long bendy backbone. As they slither along their body makes S bends. Some snakes use venom to subdue their prey. Others, such as pythons, kill by coiling around their victims and squeezing tight.

How can you tell a crocodile from an alligator?

Never smile at a crocodile

The Nile crocodile has powerful jaws armed with sharp pointed teeth. They cannot chew, but tear off chunks of flesh instead. These beads and bangle on display may have been swallowed to help the crocodile grind up food in its stomach, or was a person wearing them at the time?

You can find out about the largest reptiles that ever lived on land and in the sea on pages 7 and 24.

Beastly bite

Growing much bigger than a large dog, the Komodo dragon is the largest lizard living today. The dragon lives on islands in Indonesia. Its saliva is full of bacteria so that if a person or animal is bitten, they may die from blood poisoning.

Marine Invertebrates

Dive in to see spineless wonders from the sea.

What is a marine invertebrate?

Marine invertebrates (in-ver-ter-brates) are spineless
animals that live in the sea. Many kinds of sea animals do
not have backbones. Corals, clams, crabs, snails, starfish and
sponges are just some of these animals.

Stingers

Corals have stinging tentacles like their
relatives, the jellyfish and anemones.
These animals are called cnidaria (nye-
dare-ree-ah). Living corals are made
up of thousands of tiny anemone-like
individuals. In reef-building corals, each
individual makes
a stony cup-
like indent
in which it
lives.

Cutting and crushing

Lobsters have one pincer for crushing snails and
clams. The other pincer snips up the flesh. Lobsters
have two pairs of feelers and four pairs of walking
legs. All crustaceans have two pairs of feelers.

Not in my bath

You can use some natural bath sponges
to wash with, but this barrel sponge
would be too hard. Sponges are simple
animals with no nerves, muscles or other
tissues. They take in water and filter out
particles of food.

Meet our
scientists in the
Attenborough
Studio.

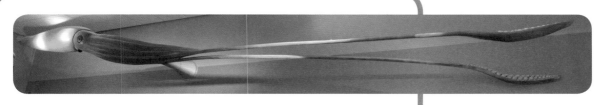

Giant of the deep

The giant squid has eyes the size of dinner plates to help it see in the dark deep ocean where it lives, as only a little light filters from the surface.

If you are 8 years or over, you can go on the Behind the Scenes Spirit Collection Tour to see a real giant squid.

You can see more crustaceans in Creepy Crawlies.

Reef watch

Can you find seven spineless animals on this reef apart from corals? Don't count the fishes, they have backbones!

Deadly beauties

If you visit a tropical reef, never pick a cone shell up. Some kinds of cone snails have a deadly sting. Snails, clams and squid are some of the soft-bodied animals that we call molluscs (moll-usks).

Minerals and The Vault

Admire minerals, meteorites, gemstones and jewels.

Find the granite in the open display of rocks. Can you see crystals of clear quartz and white feldspar?

Structure counts

The lead in your pencils is a soft mineral called graphite. The hardest mineral is diamond. Both graphite and diamond are made of pure carbon but their crystal structure is different.

Graphite mineral

Diamond

Graphite mineral

What is a mineral?

A mineral is a natural material of a particular chemical composition and crystal structure. Most rocks are made of several different kinds of mineral. For example, granite is a common rock that is chiefly made up of quartz and feldspar minerals.

Animal, vegetable or mineral?

Some substances made by living things are minerals. Stony corals make their skeletons out of the mineral calcite. Chalk is mostly calcite too. But it is made from the skeletons of tiny plant-like organisms that sank to the bottom of ancient seas.

Chalk cliffs made of tiny plant-like organisms

Gold rush

This gold nugget was found in 1853 during the Australian gold rush. Most gold is worn smooth after it has been carried away by rivers. Gold is rarely found in cube-shaped crystals like you can see here. It is usually found as small grains or gold dust.

What is a meteorite?

A meteorite is a rock from space that hits the Earth. Most meteorites are fragments of giant rocks, called asteroids. More rarely, meteorites may have come from the Moon or Mars.

Giant gem

Gemstones are beautiful minerals. They are often cut into shapes to show off their colour and sparkle. This topaz, our largest cut stone, is about the size of a pack of cards.

Count the gems

See if you can find...

5 diamonds
2 emeralds
1 amethyst
2 rubies
3 sapphires

You can see spectacular specimens and rare meteorites in The Vault.

Creepy Crawlies

Spot creepy crawlies on land, in the water and in your home.

Become a scientist and explore hundreds of real specimens in the Investigate Centre.

What is an arthropod?

Animals that creep about on jointed legs are called arthropods (ar-thro-pods). They do not have a backbone like you. Instead, their skeleton is on the outside like a suit of armour. Arthropods have to split open their skeleton to grow larger.

Sting in the tail

Like spiders, scorpions have four pairs of legs for walking. They grab prey with their pincers and swing their tail down over their head – the poisonous tip of their tail is used to stun their prey. They also use their sting to defend themselves against predators.

Who's Who?

Can you tell the four main groups of arthropods apart by counting their pairs of legs and feelers (antennae)?

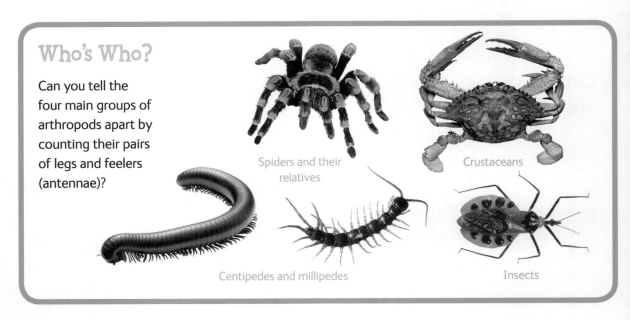

Spiders and their relatives

Crustaceans

Centipedes and millipedes

Insects

All change

Some insects go through a complete change when they grow up. A butterfly's egg hatches into a caterpillar. When fully grown, the caterpillar becomes a chrysalis. Inside the chrysalis, the caterpillar turns into a butterfly.

I am only found in the very deep waters off the coast of Japan, and can live for up to 100 years.

Long legs

The Japanese spider crab is the largest living arthropod. Its long legs are used to walk across the sea floor. When stretched out the legs measure up to 4 metres across.

Why are there so many insects?

Insects are the largest group of animals with over one million different kinds. Most insects are smaller than a 10 pence coin so there are many places where they can live. Others can be as big as a dinner plate. Can you think of other reasons why there are so many different kinds?

Fossil Marine Reptiles

Look up at the gallery walls to see fossils of monsters from the deep.

Can you see the baby ichthyosaur (ick-thee-oh-sore) being born?

Tail first

This fossil of an ichthyosaur mother shows her four babies. When the mother died, three of the babies were still inside her and the fourth had just been born tail first. Ichthyosaurs became extinct around 95 million years ago, before the dinosaurs.

What are giant marine reptiles?

Giant reptiles swam in the sea when dinosaurs roamed the land. Like all reptiles, these marine reptiles breathed air so they had to swim to the surface of the sea every so often.

Long or short necks?

Plesiosaurs had small heads and long necks. The pliosaurs had bigger heads and usually shorter necks. Both swam along using their paddle-shaped limbs to propel themselves through the water. They died out at the same time as the dinosaurs.

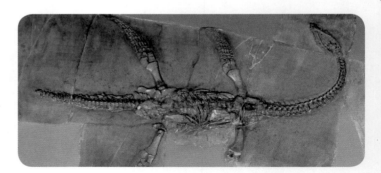

Plesiosaur (plee-zee-oh-sore)

Pliosaur (ply-oh-sore)

Find the fossil

Join the dots to find a giant marine reptile.

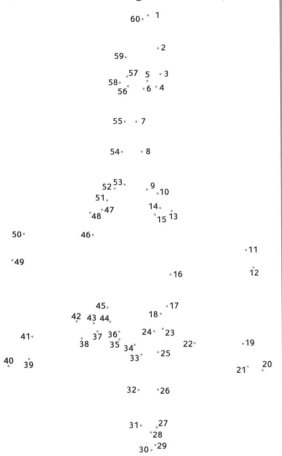

Fossil hunter

Mary Anning (1799–1847) was a whizz at finding fossils of giant marine reptiles near her home on the south coast of England. She was only 11 years old when she found her first ichthyosaur.

Sea worthy

Ichthyosaurs had a dolphin-like shape but they swam like fish with a sideways sweep of their tails. They also had two pairs of flippers for steering. The fin on their back stopped them rolling in the water.

Can you find dinosaur fossils in this gallery?

Old croc

This fossil sea crocodile lived around 180 million years ago. It caught fish with its needle-shaped teeth. Like today's saltwater crocodiles, it may have lived at the mouth of a river and swum along the coast to new places.

Birds

Seek out your finest feathered friends.

Toucans can fly

Ostriches can reach speeds of over 70 km per hour (43 mph).

Ostriches cannot fly

What is a bird?

Birds have feathers and wings, and lay hard-shelled eggs. Most birds can fly, although penguins use their wings to swim instead. Some birds, such as the ostrich and cassowary, only have tiny wings so cannot fly.

Early bird

Archaeopteryx (Ar-kee-op-ter-iks) is the earliest known bird. It lived around 147 million years ago. This peculiar bird had teeth and a long bony tail like a reptile. Unlike its feathered dinosaur ancestors, *Archaeopteryx* was able to fly.

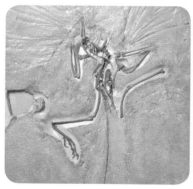

Did you know that birds are not just relatives of dinosaurs, but are dinosaurs!

Neat nests

Birds make their nests out of all kinds of stuff. The cave swiftlet makes a nest out of its spit. People collect the nests to make into soup. This weaver bird's grass nest has a long funnel-shaped entrance to stop snakes getting inside to steal the eggs.

Beaks and feet

Birds of prey, such as owls, have a hooked beak for tearing flesh and sharp talons for grabbing prey.

Colour me in

Colour in the peacock or make a note of his colours to fill in later.

Why are birds colourful?

Male birds of many different kinds have bright and colourful feathers which may help to attract a partner or alert an intruder that a territory is occupied. Females often have duller colours which make it harder for predators to spot them on their nest.

Dead as a dodo

The flightless dodo was an easy target for sailors who stopped off on the Indian Ocean island of Mauritius from the late 1500s. The sailors left pigs and rats behind that destroyed the dodos' nests and eggs. Within a hundred years, the dodo was wiped out.

Can you find a dodo on the walls inside the Museum?

Little and large

Hummingbirds lay the smallest eggs in the world. The ostrich lays the largest egg, weighing over one and a half kilos, which is about the weight of 25 chickens' eggs.

Primates

Hang out with some of your closest relatives.

What is a primate?

Primates have hands and feet that can grasp, which means they can climb trees and hang onto branches. Their eyes face forward so they can spot things in front of them and judge distances well. Most primates have nails instead of claws.

Who are you?

Primates are mammals. You are a primate! You belong to the group of primates called apes, like gibbons, orang-utans and chimpanzees. All apes (and some monkeys too) have fingernails and toenails like you. They can touch the fingers of the same hand with their thumb so they can grasp objects, like you can.

Social skills

Some primates live by themselves, such as the potto. Many others, such as squirrel monkeys and chimpanzees, live in groups. A chimp may signal to others in its group by making faces and different calls.

Which of these chimps is making a threat and which is frightened?

Find the primates

Can you find the names of these primates in the word search?

AYEAYE
BUSHBABY
CHIMPANZEE
GIBBON
GORILLA
LEMUR
LORIS
MONKEY
ORANGUTAN
POTTO
TARSIER

```
                    Z R
                    H Z
                D H E E
                P E X S
            N O B B I G
            Z M R Y D O
U G O R I L L A B E Q E J G L E M U R S
D B H O I P A O U I D Y W O E E Y G L C
D Z W S U N N S S K A L M X Z V Z G
N O J S T H H R M E O L N N C T
K F K Y S B A N Y R X A A U
O R G M A T G A I E T P
W A T O Q B N F L S B U M V
P K N T K Y Q B X W E G I O
S Q K E W O Q G Q T T M N H H Q
M E P Y V K P       Y C S A C X G
P Y Y R X H M          Y S R P T S G
J W A V C               O O V N D
U K T Y                 Y K M L
V A                     H B
```

Bringing up baby

Baby primates are helpless when born so have to be cared for by their parents. Grasping hands help a baby to cling onto its mum. Baby apes take a long time to grow up with us humans having the longest childhood. Baby monkeys are called infants, just like us.

Human DNA is nearly 99 per cent identical to chimpanzees and bonobos.

Bright and brainy

We pride ourselves on being brainy, but did you know that other primates can do clever things too? Chimpanzees can use tools, such as a twig to get termites out of a nest. They also seem to understand simple sentences made of symbols.

How we came to be

Modern humans like us evolved at least 200,000 years ago. We are survivors whereas our closest relatives, including the Neanderthals, died out. Today, chimpanzees and bonobos are our closest living relatives.

Earth Hall

Wonder at our visions of the Earth.

What is the Earth?

The Earth is one of eight planets that revolve around our star, the Sun. In ancient times, people thought the Sun revolved around the Earth. People knew little about space or even the rocks on Earth.

A marvellous mineral

Malachite is a bright green mineral that grows like a bunch of grapes, or like a stalagmite. It is a soft stone. When it is cut and polished it is one of the most beautiful gemstones, which is why it is often used for ornaments and jewellery.

Take the escalator through a giant metallic globe.

Rich resource

Iron has shaped our history from its first use in simple tools to the elegant steel bridges of today. The kidney-shaped ore you see here is 70 per cent iron. Such rich sources of iron are rare.

Discover spectacular objects in the round windows!

Devil's toenails

In the past, people thought these fossils of extinct oysters were the devil's toenails. They had no idea that seashells could be preserved in the rocks as fossils.

Moon rock

Our Moon revolves around the Earth. The piece of Moon rock inside this pyramid was brought to Earth in 1972. It is part of a 5.5 kilogramme boulder collected from the surface of the Moon by US astronauts on the Apollo 16 mission.

What is the future of the Earth?

We know more about the Earth than ever before. Yet we still have much to learn about how to use its resources wisely. We need to find a better balance between what we take and what we put back. Recycling is one way to help our planet's future.

Cars are now crushed and recycled

Word scramble

Help, our printer has gone haywire! Can you unscramble the words in our labels in the Earth Hall?

L S O F S I
B L E R A M
R A L O C H A C
A Y S C R T L
L M N I A E R

Volcanoes and Earthquakes

Feel the forces within the Earth.

Magma and lava are both molten rock. When magma reaches the surface, it is called lava.

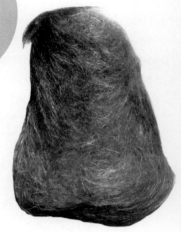

What is a volcano?

Deep within the Earth is molten rock and gas, called magma. When magma finds cracks in the surface rocks, it forces its way out as a volcano. Temperatures in a volcano can reach over 1,150°C. Some volcanoes are quiet for many years then erupt dramatically. Others spew out molten rock at frequent intervals.

Hair of a goddess

People from the Pacific Ocean island of Hawaii once believed that these strands were the hair of their volcano goddess Pele. The strands actually formed from erupting lava that has been caught by the wind.

Light as a rock!

Some molten volcanic rock is rich in gas. When it reaches the surface, the gas expands to make a rocky froth. On cooling, the froth is turned into a solid rock full of air holes, called pumice. It is normally light enough to float in water.

Nature's glass

When lava cools rapidly, its minerals have no time to form crystals. The sharp, glassy rock made is called obsidian (ob-sid-ee-an).

Moving plates

The Earth is made of gigantic plates that take millions of years to drift across its surface. In some places, such as along the floor of the Atlantic Ocean, molten rock comes out and forces the plates apart. In other places, plates collide and one may move under the other, down into the Earth's molten interior.

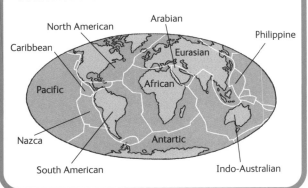

What is an earthquake?

Earthquakes are the shaking forces that mostly come from movements of the Earth's plates. In March 2011, an earthquake hit Japan's northeast coast. Sadly, 15,370 people were killed as buildings fell down and as the tsunami, triggered by the earthquake, swept over the land.

Experience the earthquake – the force of the real quake would be many times greater

What comes from where? For help see page 36.

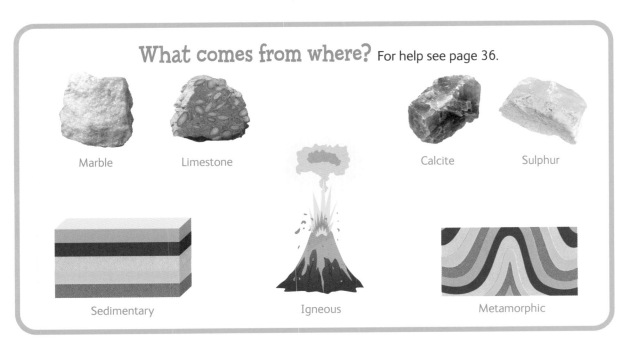

Marble

Limestone

Calcite

Sulphur

Sedimentary

Igneous

Metamorphic

Restless Surface

Dig into the Earth's ever-changing surface.

Discover how ancient life makes limestone.

What is weathering?

Surface rocks are under constant attack. They can be broken down by acidic chemicals in rain like this limestone gargoyle. They can also be broken up by physical forces. For example, when water in a crack freezes, it expands and may shatter rock.

Carried away

Loose rocks are carried away and eroded by water, wind and ice. The odd-shaped rock has been blasted by wind and rain that have removed the softer layers – this is known as weathering. The oval boulder has been transported in water. Its sharp edges have been worn away by bashing into other rocks and the river bed as it rolled along.

How different do these rocks feel to touch?

Do you know the name for a feature growing down from the roof of a cave?

Mites go up

Over hundreds of years, mineral-rich water dripping onto the floor of a limestone cave makes a stalagmite.

Patterns in the sand

On the beach you may see how a stream flowing out to sea makes channels in the sand. What patterns can you make in our sand table?

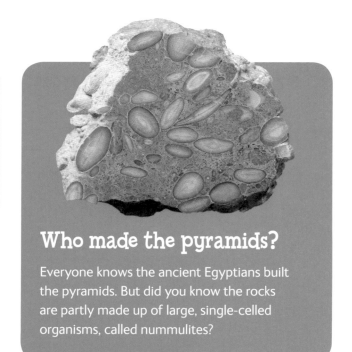

Who made the pyramids?

Everyone knows the ancient Egyptians built the pyramids. But did you know the rocks are partly made up of large, single-celled organisms, called nummulites?

Get sorted

Sand, pebbles and even shells are picked up and carried along by moving water. When the water slows down, it drops the larger material first. Strong currents moved these shells into a heap millions of years ago, then sand and mud dropped on top of them.

What helps to wear away mountains?

Fill in the puzzle to reveal the answer in the shaded squares.

1. What are rocks made of?
2. What planet do we live on?
3. What fossil fuel is made of woody material?
4. What grows up from the floor of a cave?
5. What expands in cracks to shatter rocks?
6. What do we call life forms turned into rocks?
7. What living animals helped to build the pyramids?

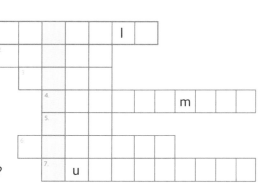

Earth's Treasury

Unlock the treasures from the rocks.

What is a rock?

There are three main types of rocks. Igneous rocks, like granite, form from molten rock. Sedimentary rocks, like sandstone, form from other rocks, the remains of living things and from mineral crystallization. Metamorphic rocks, like gneiss, are rocks changed deep in the Earth by heat and pressure.

Superman's super enemy

Our scientists were amazed to discover a new mineral in Serbia that has the same chemical composition as the kryptonite in the film, *Superman Returns*. Kryptonite is the only substance that can weaken Superman. The new mineral is actually called jadarite.

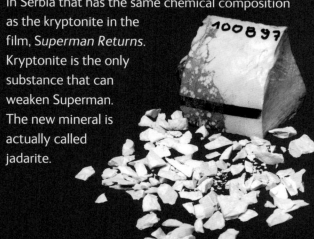

Double vision

Minerals have different properties. If you look through a crystal of the mineral calcite you will see things in double. As light rays go through the crystal, they are split in two. Try looking through the huge crystal in the gallery.

Glow in the dark

We cannot see ultraviolet (UV) light. But shine UV light on some kinds of minerals, and you can see them glow in the dark like this fluorite and willemite. The minerals take in UV light then emit the energy in colours you can see.

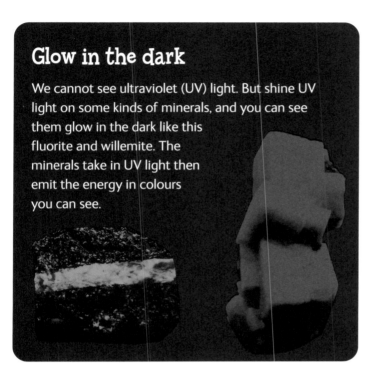

Useful metals

Metals taken from the rocks can be made into many things. See if you can fill in the missing words. Can you find the answers in the gallery?

Silver is made into   _ _ w _ _ _ _ _ y

Copper is made into   _ i _ i _ _

Iron is made into   _ _ e e _

Lead is made into   r _ _ _ i _ _

Fuel from rocks

Can you name another type of fossil fuel in the gallery?

Oil is the remains of tiny plants and animals that lived in lakes and the sea. The remains sank to the bottom of the sea and were covered by layers of mud and sand. The weight of the layers above turned the remains into oil.

Why is sand so useful?

Grains of sand are tiny fragments of rock. Sand is mostly made of the common mineral quartz, which you can see sometimes as a big crystal. Quartz is made of silicon and oxygen. Pure quartz sand is used to make computer chips, glass, ceramics and sandpaper.

From the Beginning

You can find out about meteorites on page 21.

Trek through time.

How old is the Earth?

Scientists can tell how old the Earth is by studying meteorites. Unlike rocks on Earth, the oldest meteorites have not changed since the solar system was formed. The solar system (including the Earth) is about 4,560 million years old. This meteorite is made of debris left after the solar system formed. The Museum's collection contains approximately 2,000 individual meteorites.

Rock rust

Scientists can find clues about early life on Earth by looking at rocks. The reddish bands in this 3,000 million-year-old rock contain iron combined with oxygen-like rust. Scientists believe that the oxygen was made by the Earth's first plant-like organisms.

In the sea

Around 545 million years ago, a variety of animals lived in the sea. Some animals were soft and squishy like jellyfish. Others had hard parts such as shells and outer skeletons. Many of these early animals, including trilobites, became extinct about 248 million years ago.

Look for trilobites and other sea fossils in Fossils in Britain.

What are fossils?

Fossils are rock-like materials that show evidence of animals or plants that lived millions of years ago. They can tell us many things about the past and have been found on every continent of the Earth. Can you find out how fossils are formed?

First life forms

Tiny fossils show that there were chains of simple cells living on Earth 3,500 million years ago.

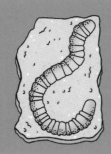

Follow the gallery's timeline, each metre equals 25 million years!

First fishes

The first fishes had no jaws at all. Around 400 million years ago, fishes with jaws began to appear. This huge fish had jaws and lived about 90 million years ago.

Stepping onto land

The first four-legged animals clambered onto land about 375 million years ago. Like amphibians today, they bred in water. Reptiles, like this *Bradysaurus*, an early plant-eater, were the first to lay eggs on land. This reptile was about 2.5 metres long.

Strange remains

Mammals did well after the dinosaurs died out about 66 million years ago. Among the mammals, humans were recent arrivals with people like us appearing at least 200,000 years ago. From about 50,000 years ago, human hunters began to kill off many kinds of large animals like the ground sloth.

Incredible Collections

Stored behind the scenes are all sorts of bizarre and beautiful objects.

What is in store?

We have over 80 million objects in store with around 150,000 more added each year. Specimens are kept in the main Museum, the Darwin Centre and the Natural History Museum at Tring.

Our specimens include about

- 28 million insects
- 27 million other animals
- 9 million fossils
- 6 million plants
- 1 million birds
- 500,000 rocks and minerals
- 3,200 meteorites

We use flesh-eating beetles and their larvae to strip flesh from bones for storage.

Thanks Sir Hans

Sir Hans Sloane (1660–1753), a doctor, gathered together tens of thousands of plants, animals, gemstones, coins and ancient objects during his life from other collectors and his own collecting. When he died they were bought and displayed in the British Museum. In the late 1800s the natural history objects were moved to our Museum.

Beetles

Charles Darwin (1809–1882) was a famous scientist who put forward ideas of how living things can change through time. We have some of his collections including this beetle on the left from Chile, which nipped his finger.

Wet, dry and frozen

Some of our animal specimens are kept in jars of fluid. Others are kept dry, such as shells, skeletons and skins. We also keep frozen tissue and DNA from endangered animals. If one of these became extinct, the frozen material would give us valuable information about the animal.

Set in stone

Scientists study fossils in rocks to understand the history of life on Earth. They remove the bits of rock with a hammer and chisel. Then they may use

acids, or fire hard pellets at the rock. Finally, they remove the last grains of rock using a dentist's drill, scalpels and needles.

Learn about the diversity of life by visiting the interactive gallery in the Darwin Centre's Cocoon.

State of the art facilities

Collections, scientists and visitors come together in the Darwin Centre. It houses the animal, plant and insect collections, and high-tech science labs. You can see the scientists at work and take a closer look at the collections.

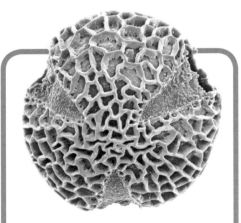

Little and large

Pollen grains are some of the tiniest things in store. They are usually kept on microscope slides. The largest specimen is the skeleton of the blue whale hanging in Hintze Hall.

Super Science

Our scientists are discovering more about the natural world.

Discover the amazing variety of creatures living in the Wildlife Garden pond.

What do our scientists do?

The Museum has over 350 scientists. They study the collections to understand the variety of life. New species are discovered by comparing specimens with those already identified in our collections.

Martian meteorites

The Museum has 12 fragments of some 75 Martian meteorites that have been discovered on Earth. Studying the meteorites gives us clues as to what Mars was like in the past.

What is a person who studies meteorites called? Meteorologist or meteoriticist?

First Brits

Our scientists were part of a team that discovered early people lived in Britain about 800,000 years ago. When ice sheets spread across Britain, these early peoples either died out or moved south. Others then returned when it was warmer. About 12,000 years ago, our ancestors were able to settle in Britain for good.

See the first adult Neanderthal skull ever found in Human Evolution.

Deadly diseases

Tiny worms infect over 200 million people. If an infected person pees or poos in a lake, the worms can be picked up by snails. The worms multiply in the snails and when shed into the water can infect other people. Museum scientists are studying the worms and snails to find ways to control them.

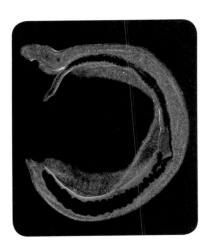

Tracking mozzies

There are certain kinds of mosquitoes that carry malaria, which is a disease that kills over one million people throughout the world each year. Our scientists are finding new ways to identify the dangerous mosquitoes by identifying bits of their DNA (genes).

Plant protection

The xaté (sha-tay) palm is used in flower arrangements because the cut stems last for a long time. Museum scientists helped to find ways to protect the palm, which is illegally harvested from forests in Belize, South America.

Stranded whales

The Museum records whales and dolphins that have come ashore around Britain. Some have died at sea before being washed up on the beach. Others have swum ashore by mistake and then died. Sadly, many whales and dolphins die after being caught in fishing gear.

More about the Museum

Discover more fascinating facts.

Is it real?

Not all the specimens you see in our displays are real. Some are models or casts made from the real thing. Soft parts are usually removed because they rot. So you can see dry bones, shells and stuffed specimens. Some fishes are stuffed too, others are models or pickled in fluid.

Spot the real bits

Look at the hippopotamus model in the Mammals gallery. Which bits of the hippo are real?

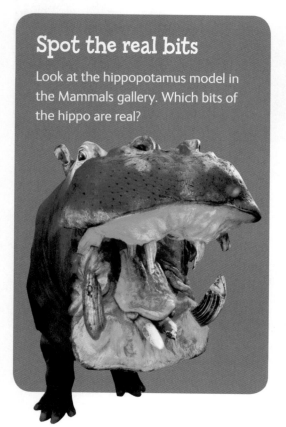

Rhinos are often killed by poachers for their horns. The ones on display are all fake.

Old collections

Most of the animals you see in the Museum were collected many years ago. This is why some of them look faded. Today, we do not take animals from the wild just for a display. Some of the animals are now endangered, such as the black rhinoceros.

Dust busters

Over the years, dust settles on anything not kept inside a case. We have a team of dust busters, called conservationists, who keep our specimens clean. They use special vacuum cleaners, dusters and brushes to carefully remove the dust. One of their biggest jobs is to clean the blue whale.

Party time

When the last visitor has left, the Museum is not as quiet as you may think. Some nights, huge parties are held in the Hintze Hall like this Dino Snores party. Parties help us to raise money to support the Museum's work.

Helping the planet

The Museum is trying to help the planet by using less energy. We have a power plant that uses waste heat from electricity generation to keep the Museum warm, and meters keep a check on how much electricity is used on every floor.

Did you know that using disposable items like drinks bottles, coffee cups and packaging creates a lot of unnecessary rubbish that can pollute our land, seas and rivers if we're not careful? Help reduce the amount of rubbish we create by bringing your reusable water bottle with you to the Museum. You can refill it for free at water bottle refill points all around the Museum. Find them on the map marked with this symbol 🚰

Answers

p2 Q: *What other features make it look like a cathedral?*
A: Pillars, stained glass, high ceiling, gilded panels.

p5 Q: *How many of these clay creatures can you spot inside and outside the Museum?* A: Bat (top of some pillars in the Museum Shop); kangaroo (above the Museum's main entrance); lion (roof on the left wing as you face the entrance); monkey (on the arches in the Hintze Hall); octopus (near the bottom of some pillars in the *Dinosaurs* gallery); owl (on the top of some pillars in the *Dinosaurs* gallery – best seen from the walkway); pterosaur (outside on the right wing as you face the entrance).

p5 Q: *The tree was a seedling in the year 557. How old was the tree when it was cut down in 1892?* A: The redwood was cut down when it was 1,335 years old!

p7 *Allosaurus, Baryonyx, Coelophysis, Deinocheirus, Edmontosaurus, Fukuiraptor, Gallimimus, Hypsilophodon, Iguanodon, Janenschia, Kentrosaurus, Lambeosaurus, Maiasaura, Nedoceratops, Oviraptor, Pachycephalosaurus, Quaesitosaurus, Rugops, Saltopus, Tyrannosaurus, Utahraptor, Velociraptor, Wintonotitan, Xiaotingia, Yinlong, Zalmoxes*

p9 Match the heads
1. *Oviraptor*; 2. *Baryonyx*; 3. *Euoplocephalus*

p10 Q: *What kind of joint lets you bend at the knees?*
A: A hinge joint.

p10 Q: *Can you hear a baby's heartbeat when it is in its mother's womb?*
A: Yes you can hear the baby's heartbeat.

p11 Q: *What do you see?* A: 1. You may see this as both a duck and a rabbit. 2. The lines drawn trick our brain as only parts of the object are in 3D. 3. Both lines are the same length.

p13 Q: *Match the mammal to where it lives.*
A: Sloth, South American rainforest; jerboa, Sahara desert; lion, African grassland; capybara, South American swamp; snow leopard, Himalayan mountains.

p13 Q: *What is the proper name for a mammal that has a pouch?* A: Marsupial.

p14 Odds on
Q: *Fill in the names of some odd-toed hoofed mammals.*

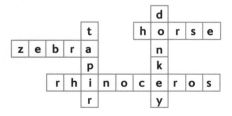

p16 Spot the difference A: Sea turtles, such as the leatherback turtle, have flattened shells, which make them more streamlined, and flippers. Tortoises have domed shells and legs for walking.

p16 Spot the difference

p17 Q: *How can you tell a crocodile from an alligator?*
A: When the crocodile's jaws are shut, you can see the fourth tooth in its lower jaw. In the alligator (and caiman) the tooth is hidden because the fourth tooth slots into a pit in the upper jaw.

p19 Q: *Can you find 7 spineless animals apart from corals on this coral reef?* A: Jellyfish; cone snail; giant clam; lobster; starfish; sea urchin; sea anemone.

p22 Q: *Can you tell the four main groups of arthropods apart by counting their pairs of legs and feelers (antennae)?*
A: Spiders and their relatives have four pairs of legs and no feelers. Crustaceans have two pairs of feelers. Centipedes have one pair of legs on each segment of their body and millipedes have two pairs of legs on each segment. Millipedes usually have more pairs of legs than centipedes but never have 1,000 legs. They have one pair of feelers. Insects have three pairs of legs and one pair of feelers.

p23 Q: *Why are there so many insects?*
A: Insects live in freshwater, on land and in the sea. Insects do not need to eat much to stay alive. Insects breed quickly and can adapt to new conditions.

p25 Q: *Can you find dinosaur fossils in this gallery?*
A: Plesiosaurs, ichthyosaurs and other giant marine reptiles were not dinosaurs. Did you spot the slab of rock with a fossil *Stegosaurus* dinosaur in this gallery?

p25 Find the fossil
A: The pliosaur *Rhomaleosaurus*, which has a long neck.

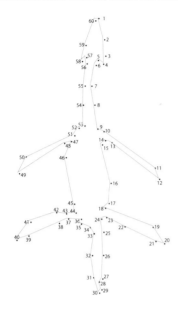

p27 Q: *Can you find a dodo on the walls of the Museum?*
A: In the *Minerals* gallery above a door to the left of *The Vault*.

p28 Q: *Which of these chimps is making a threat and which is frightened?* A: Chimp with pursed lips is making a threat. Chimp baring its teeth is frightened.

p29 Find the primates

p31 Word scramble
A: FOSSIL, MARBLE, CHARCOAL, CRYSTAL, MINERAL.

p33 What comes from where

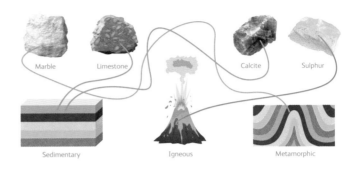

Marble   Limestone   Calcite   Sulphur

Sedimentary   Igneous   Metamorphic

p34 Q: *Do you know the name for a feature growing down from the roof of a cave?*
A: Stalactite.

p35 Q: *What helps to wear away mountains?*

m	i	n	e	r	a	l	s			
	e	a	r	t	h					
	c	o	a	l						
	s	t	a	l	a	g	m	i	t	e
	i	c	e							
f	o	s	s	i	l	s				
	n	u	m	m	u	l	i	t	e	s

p37 Q: *Can you name another type of fossil fuel in the gallery?* A: Coal.

p37 Useful metals
Silver is made into jewellery
Copper is made into wiring
Iron is made into steel
Lead is made into roofing

p42 Q: *What is a person who studies meteorites called?* A: Meteoriticist. A meteorologist studies the weather.

p44 Spot the real bits
A: Eyes are made of glass, ears are real, skin is real, teeth are real, tongue is a model.

What is your favourite thing in the Natural History Museum?

Draw a picture or stick in a photograph of you and your favourite thing.

© The Trustees of the Natural History Museum, London, 2017. All rights reserved. Reprinted 2018, reprinted with updates 2019, 2022.

ISBN 978 0 565 094171

10 9 8 7 6 5

The Author has asserted her right to be identified as the Author of this work under the Copyright, Designs and Patents Act 1988.

Author: Dr Miranda MacQuitty based on some original concepts developed by Nick Ives and Margarita Petri
Designer: Bobby Birchall
Illustrator: Jo Moore
Reproduction: Saxon Digital Services
Printer: Printer Trento Srl, Italy

Photo credits: p1. ©pookpiik/istockphoto.com (bottom), ©ShaunWilkinson/istockphoto.com (top); p.2 ©CoreyFord/istockphoto.com (bottom right); p.4 © Piotr Krzeslak/istockphoto.com (top), ©GlobalP/istockphoto.com (middle); p.5, 26 (top) ©istockphoto.com; p.6, 7, 10, 19, 21, 25, 29, 33, 39 ©Jo Moore Illustrations; p.8, 27 (top), 28 (top left) ©John Sibbick (top); p.12 f9photos/istockphoto.com (top); p.13 ©istockphoto.com (sloth, snow leopard, rainforest, swamp, capybara); p.13 © Daniel Heuclin/NHPA (jerboa); p.13© Getty Images (grassland, mountains, lion, Sahara); p.14 ©Hanne & Jens Eriksen/naturepl.com (left); p.19 ©istockphoto.com (middle left); p.26 ©USO/istockphoto.com; p.28 ©GAPS/istockphoto.com (bottom); p.32 ©Zephyr/Science Photo Library (middle left); p.34 ©Tony Waltham Geophotos (middle right); p.37 CostinT/istockphoto.com (bottom right); p.37 ©benjamin fontaine/fotalia; p.38 ©stray_cat/istockphoto.com.
All other images © The Trustees of the Natural History Museum, London.

Every effort has been made to contact all copyright holders. If we have been unsuccessful we apologize and welcome correction for future editions and reprints.

Keep in touch

Join our membership. Visit the website: http://www.nhm.ac.uk/support-us/membership.html

Natural History Museum,
Cromwell Road, London SW7 5BD

T +44 (0)207 942 5000

Opening times:
Monday–Sunday 10:00–17:50

Entrance is free!

For all activity times and prices please ask a member of staff or see display boards.

 facebook.com/naturalhistorymuseum
 instagram.com/natural_history_museum
 twitter.com/NHM_London
 youtube.com/naturalhistorymuseum

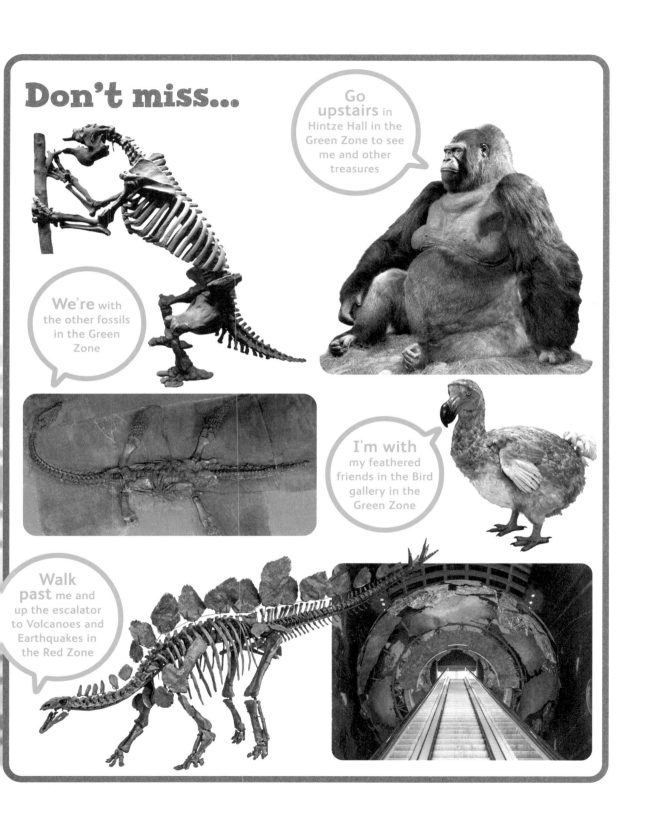

Don't miss...

Go **upstairs** in Hintze Hall in the Green Zone to see me and other treasures

We're with the other fossils in the Green Zone

I'm with my feathered friends in the Bird gallery in the Green Zone

Walk past me and up the escalator to Volcanoes and Earthquakes in the Red Zone